Words to Feel

Jacqueline Thompson

BALBOA.PRESS

A DIVISION OF HAY HOUSE

Balboa Press books may be ordered through booksellers or by contacting:

Balboa Press
A Division of Hay House
1663 Liberty Drive
Bloomington, IN 47403
www.balboapress.com.au
1 (877) 407-4847

Print information available on the last page.

ISBN: 978-1-5043-2039-9 (sc)
ISBN: 978-1-5043-2040-5 (e)

Balboa Press rev. date: 02/07/2020

Contents

Introduction

I would like to introduce myself personally
with these words that follow.

Words

You, my friend, are my audience
The words I write are my connection to you
Connections through heart and soul
Blessed to be able to express my inner most thoughts and feelings
With only love in my heart
These words will depart

Child

You are the child that needs to be listened to you have a
uniqueness in this world that only you have and that is you
It is yours it is your smile your laughter your sadness
even the way you tie your shoes or wear your hat
That is you peeping under that brim never deny that the
sparkle in your eye is there because being a child is a special
part of life from your dirty clothes and your messy hair.
I want you to love you and all that you do hold this in
your heart and it will always be there, love you so much
that there is always a little more love to share.

Always

I was always trying to do the right thing I was
always giving away love that made peoples hearts sing I was
only just a child learning everyday how to laugh runaround
joke and play you didn't know it that some would react
differently to your antics and to your party not come
I did sweet in every way and couldn't understand why they
wouldn't want to play I was yet to find the uniqueness
in my soul. I was yet to find the complicated ways in
growing old. I have held on and not let life take me
down I am still beautiful and wonderful and still me. A
little older a little sweeter a little wiser but still me

Change

Beauty before us a land, a world so dear
What we have done here I dread and fear
we can now grow from here
Change our ways
To bring peace to our earth for the rest of our days

Moving On

Clearing my thoughts I'm moving on
The past is the past and the new era has begun
A time for understanding a time for forgiving a
time for moving onto new beginnings

A Chance

Come together and build our strength as friends
See today as the beginning not the end
A chance to rewrite the story
Another chance to get it right.
Another chance to start over,
to say we will and not we might.
In all that we do in all that we say
We have a new chance to get it right with every passing day.

Voices

Confusion some days sets in
Not a good way for my day to begin
I can feel this now
So from the quiet voices that guide me through my day
Show me how I should play
So only good will come my way

Diamonds

Diamonds glisten on a clear morning
everyday with the new dawning
The pristine Blue Lake
The birds in flight
The overpowering disposition of beauty and quiet

Friend

Here I stand in peace my friend with all
the love in my heart to send
To you and hope it finds it's way
To find you in good health and hope
you're having a wonderful day
I think of you quite often because the distances are far
So hope the love finds you with love
Exactly where you are

Thankful

I am so thankful for what I have always
with the opportunity to grow
What life has in front of me I am yet to know.
This holds excitement for me as I go through
every day to sew my seeds
for growth, love, hope and happiness along the way
with only myself to please with every passing day.

Coming Together

I have searched all my life for the beautiful in everyone
not always finding what I was looking for
I keep searching I keep searching
I live in hope that one day we will unite and
with strength win our wordly plight.
We are coming together as one
with hope with love always love in our hearts
in the souls of the old and the young
A world at peace a world with unity a world enveloped by love,
I keep searching I keep searching
Will this ever be enough

Humble

I linger within the harmony of nature and
it sounds of peace and tranquility
oh so humble in the space that surrounds and calms me

Our Land

I live on this land and it's the best part of my life right now.
It is so glorious and I sit in wonder and ponder in its beauty
surrounding me, involving me in all it has to offer to my being
right here, right now and forever thankful

I Have Loved You

I sit here crying wondering when all this pain will come to an end
so I decided to put it in words and let myself be heard
if only you could help me the way that I have helped you
if only you could see just exactly what I do for you
if only you could feel in your heart the
way I feel we would never depart
I have loved you from the day we met
I have loved you from the day I held your hand
all the things we had planned seemed to come
to us like a story written in the sand
I have loved you, I have loved you
I look back now and see
that I have loved you more and in doing this I had lost me.
The true me

Nature's Beauty

Here in the peace and quiet
watching the animals at play and the birds in flight.
I feel blessed that this is all for me
with nature's beauty as far as the eye can see.
I am so at peace with nothing but what I hear for company.
It is pure pristine and glorious to behold as I
sit in anticipation as the day unfolds.

Contentment

In daylight with nothing but quiet
I watch the clouds drift on by
and the different colours playing with my eyes.
From the green of the trees and the blue of the sky
to the brown of the Earth it all makes me smile
all this for me to share
with anyone who can see
that it's this simple beauty in life that we all need.

Abundance

Life offers you more
so my friend I start opening doors
On my journey to find new things to explore
to open my eyes and move me forward
so I can be where I can truly see
life and the explosion of beauty and abundance around me

Soulful Music

Music makes my heart and soul dance
It's like finding a new love, a sweet new romance,
Finding new peace in all it does for me
The lightness I feel it's just
Pure glory and now all that I need

Always Home

To walk a meditation on its own
to just put on your shoes and roam
over the grass and through the trees
to feel contented and at ease
to be free in nature to do as I please
How I would love to find new places to roam and
feel that freedom of always feeling like home

Within My Heart

Tranquility and peace
Makes my life complete
It moves in mysterious ways
It takes over my Body and Soul and this is where it plays
It creates a light
A zest for life
A love from within that never departs
A love that finds a permanent home within
my being and within my heart

Chances

Come together and build our strength as friends
see today as the beginning not the end
A chance to rewrite the story
another chance to get it right.
Another chance to start over,
to say we will and not we might.
In all that we do in all that we say
we have a new chance to get it right with every passing day.

Rain

The rain falls
And I listen to the sounds off nature soothing me as
this wonder renews life to our dusty existence.
So much beauty it will bring forth
it's like the tears in your eyes,
that soulful cleanse that is needed every now and then.
So rain

Say it

It's you who controls your happiness
It's you who controls the tears
It's a strength given to all of us
To conquer our own heart's fears
So please don't listen to the negative that you hear
Say I am loved, say I am blessed
Say that the others don't have to like it because
I find comfort in my own glorious mess
Say it over and over so it becomes clear that the only
acceptance you need for you, is from you
The only voice you need to pay attention to
The only voice you need to hear

Shape You're In

You are my friend from now till my journey's end
I think of how blessed I am to have you as my friend
We thrive on love and all the things in between
There's times when I thought hey you are very
angry my friend, and that was a little mean
But a friend you are through thick and thin, through
happy and sad, through stress and sin
That's what a friend's about knowing that love takes many shapes
No matter what kind of shape you're in
So buckle up my friend because you're along for the ride
Knowing that there's a safe place in your
heart and always by your side

Flowers

The flowers so sweet in colour and perfume
Enhances the moment as I walk into the room
It fills the air that surrounds and lifts the
moment in the serenity that's found
In an aroma that lifts your spirit and lights your soul
Relax, breathe now and let this feeling unfold

To Dream

I think now of being a child
Good memories of simple ways
Not a concern about life overall
And nothing to complicate your days
Do you ever wonder how it good it could be
To uncomplicate our lives with this child like mentality
To love everything and everybody in your day
Not a concern about life overall and to just play
It sounds simple I know
To just remember what I did as a child and to dream of better ways
To make life beautiful
To uncomplicate our world and continue dreaming of better days